THE INK CLOUD READER

Kit Fan is a poet, novelist and critic born and educated in Hong Kong before moving to the UK at twenty-one. His first poetry collection, *Paper Scissors Stone* (2011), won the Hong Kong University International Poetry Prize. *As Slow as Possible* (2018) was a Poetry Book Society Recommendation and one of the *Irish Times* Books of the Year. He was shortlisted twice for the *Guardian* 4th Estate BAME Short Story Prize. He won the Northern Writers Awards for Fiction and for Poetry, the *Times* Stephen Spender Poetry Translation Prize, and *Poetry Magazine* Editors' Prize for Reviewing. His debut novel is *Diamond Hill* (2021). *The Ink Cloud Reader* is his third poetry collection. He was elected Fellow of the Royal Society of Literature in 2022.

ALSO BY KIT FAN

Poetry

Paper Scissors Stone

As Slow As Possible

Fiction

Diamond Hill

The Ink Cloud Reader

KIT FAN

CARCANET POETRY

First published in Great Britain in 2023 by
Carcanet
Alliance House, 30 Cross Street
Manchester, M2 7AQ
www.carcanet.co.uk

A CIP catalogue record for this book is available from the British Library.

ISBN 978 1 80017 314 9

Cover Image & Images in the Book © Kit Fan
Book design by LiteBook Prepress Services
Printed in Great Britain by SRP Ltd, Exeter, Devon

MIX
Paper from responsible sources
FSC® C014540
FSC www.fsc.org

The publisher acknowledges financial assistance from Arts Council England.

Supported using public funding by
ARTS COUNCIL ENGLAND

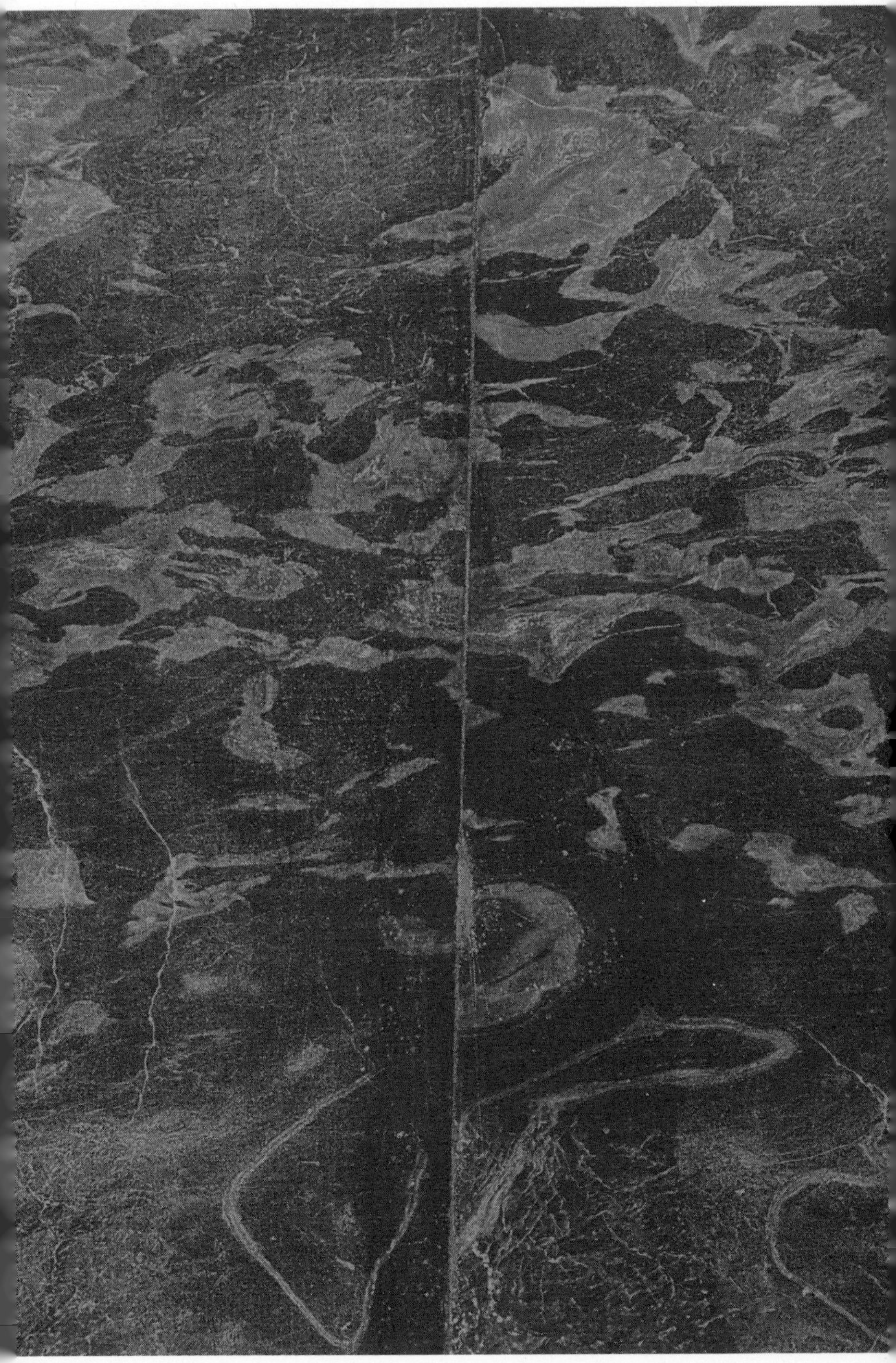

Once, a Chinese Literature
and Calligraphy teacher told me
a story. She had a reputation
in the school: nobody ever saw her
smile, inside or outside
the classroom, not even once.
People said she didn't have
the muscles in her face to move
the mouth upwards.
We were practising calligraphy.
We always did that in the height
of summer, in the afternoon,
in a classroom over thirty students,
without air-con, with only two fans
spinning overhead. I had an ink
stone and an ink stick made
with soot, animal glue
and sometimes incense.
I grounded the ink stick on the ink
stone with water to make ink.
It sounded romantic but it wasn't.
We could have bought ink
in plastic bottles. It was pointless
and messy, ink on my table,
fingers, white shirt and face.
One afternoon, out of the blue
she started telling us a story,
a story about Wang Xizhi,
probably the greatest calligrapher
in China.
Wang was born in the Jin Dynasty,
around Fourth Century AD.
He was a talented boy
at a very young age and was taught
by Lady Wei, a very demanding
teacher. Whenever Wang Xizhi
made a mistake (it could be
the stroke slightly too curved,
tilted, long or short), he was ordered
to clean his ink brush in the pond
outside the classroom.
Wang made many mistakes
and had to wash his brush
thousands of times. Day after day,
month after month, the pond
darkened and darkened.
It became an ink pond.
We were practising calligraphy
and she asked us to imagine
what Wang Xizhi would have seen
in his ink pond. Would he have seen
the towering storm clouds
we now call cumulonimbus?
Would he have seen the trees
fidgeting in the wind?
Would he have seen the inky
goldfishes in the pond?
Would he have seen himself
in the ink-surface that had turned into
a mirror?

FOR HUGH

‘if a thing happens once
it happens once for ever’

DEREK MAHON

CONTENTS

BROKEN NOSED JIZŌ

THE INK CLOUD READER

CUMULONIMBUS

Halfway through my life
the reeds by Meguro River
where the ducks made love
stop whistling. I fear I've over-
inked, or the linseed oil
soured the sky. The wind
tastes of oysters grilled
over autumn soil.
A fish draws a ripple,
or did a raindrop win?
My papers will topple
the house before the tin
roof falls. I'd better make haste
and find a new address.
A long-legged fly by the watercress
skates upstream, brazen-faced.
What I need now, to change
the half-course of my life,
is to be struck by lightning
and survive it, like Hokusai.

ONCE UPON A CLOUD

Sometimes we see a cloud that's dragonish

Shakespeare

SUDDENLY

Never use 'suddenly', the most overused, least-needed word in fiction.
– Elmore Leonard

Suddenly, the cloud-knots unravelled and a droplet fell
from a womb. Three days of hard labour had broken
her. She said she was too tired to name the boy.

Suddenly, the blackened milk teeth gave up after a year
of antibiotics. The doctors were baffled. His locked mouth was fed
swifts' solidified saliva to clear his feverish chest.

Home left him suddenly.

At a zebra crossing, his father suddenly took his hand.
No cars, no danger ahead, but being held was a strange thing.
Moving in with his family, stranger.

Suddenly, first week at school he stopped speaking.
Teacher called his mother in. When asked to explain
the silence, he said he had nothing to say.

Suddenly at 14, on a bridge, he vowed never to reproduce.

Desire suddenly overtook fear. After watching Kieslowski's *Dekalog* in one sitting he spelt out his heart and asked what togetherness meant. Joe walked off in the rain.

Years later, suddenly, he discovered from the *Book of Not*: not watching *Dekalog*, not asking the right question, not spelling things out, no Joe and no rain.

Suddenly, a handful of milk-seeds, and suddenly, men…

Suddenly 2001. Two professors persuaded him to study a malleable thing called literature. Hong Kong had returned to China but he flew to Britain.

Suddenly, people spoke Yorkshire. Luv on the bus. Luv in the shops. Yorkshire stared at him and he stared back, two neurons in a busy translation loop.

Suddenly, one autumn, he found love and blockades.

A logjam and suddenly diversions. Everywhere the road
signs read Divorce, Teenagers, Anorexia. He claimed driving
was in his DNA because his father was a taxi driver.

Suddenly, his tongue tripped on the English alphabet
as he rebuilt the Telford Gardens Library he'd been brought up in
but now demolished. People called that poetry.

Suddenly, a voice, a temporary abode.

Suddenly he failed, and blamed the words
and the swifts' saliva. How many edible bird nests were robbed
in exchange for a lottery of half-tuned stolen keys?

And what could he say to the superior blast
that suddenly erased his vocal cords, retinas, eardrums, taste buds,
and all the tensions on his fingertips, tendons, heart?

Suddenly, rain churns up the clouds. And, stops.

IF
time is heat
travelling
from hot
to cold
when is
the hour
date
location
of my death
?
Would I be
accompanied
?
Someone
holding
my hand
putting a bitter
mint in my
mouth
?
Would
morphine be
administered
?
How cold
could my toes
get before
they fall off
?
Would there
be a setting
sun
?

IF
my severed
head
were to be
frozen
could I still
retrieve
a memory
file
from 24th
August 2017
the swim I had
with Hugh
by the harbour
in Trani and
the Michelin-
starred dinner
that followed
?
Would it be
possible to
relish
the handmade
tagliatelle with
langoustines
again
?
Or the risotto
nero
?
How much
would the
access
cost
?

IF
I were to be
cast away
in the river
of blood
in the Seventh
Circle with
the citizens
of Sodom
and Gomorrah
would my
husband
be there
?
What
equipment
if any could
withstand
the barren
plain
of sand ignited
by the flakes
of fire
?
Would
the guards
take bribes
?
Would the fact
that we were
both decent
swimmers
help
?

IF
against the
odds I were
reincarnated
as a Japanese
maple
Higasayama
what would
stop me
from being
turned into
a bonsai tree
?
And IF
I cohabited
well with
the aphids
and bull-
finches
would I be
personified
in the next
cycle
?
What sins
should I
accumulate
to avoid being
human
again
?

IF
in the end
there is
nothingness
not even
the ink
and the clouds
would nothing
then be left
of me
?
What would
happen
to the books
I read
and the books
I wrote
?
Would
the memory
of the pages
I loved and
the memory
of my pages
loved by
others
fade away
equally
in the light-
years of
reading
?

IF
what you told
Oribasius
is true and
the speaking
water
has been
silenced
why are the
seas rising
?
Why do we
have more
kings
with splendid
halls
sprouting
high from
the ground
?
And IF
Phoebus
has lost
his house and
the laurel's
tongue
is cut
why am I
here
?
What are
the words
that can never
be
silenced
?

YEW

You walk into the dark heart of the yew
to stop the cells from dividing like the dew.
The yew walks intravenously into you
tightening the microtubules like a screw
and all your internal scaffolding once alive and askew
turns rigid, indivisible. It's the body's haiku
to rot and blossom, overthrowing us in a coup
that ends in soil or fire. You walk into the yew
for a second chance, for an alternative avenue.
And the yew walks soundlessly into you
as your hair thins out, muscles soften to tofu
and your lips turn metallic blue.
Soon we will walk together to Peru or Timbuktu
but first you must walk alone in the mind of the yew.

THE CHARACTERS Sun, Shade, Yew, Sick Man, Another Man, Book

ACT I *Outside Malton Community Hospital. Urology Department. Now and then, by a yew hedge, the sun flits around.*

SUN: I prefer shade.

SHADE: (*rolling into a leaf*) Please take the yew.

SUN: (*turning bright electric blue*) Are you afraid? (*The shade jumps and transforms into a seagull landing on a terracotta chimney. It's the Eighth of June. Everywhere speaks Being and Cloudlessness. The pair argue in sunlight and shadow, mostly subdued, while a white ambulance pulls into a parking bay unloading a man onto a metal frame that moves and shines like the sun.*)

SHADE: I'm sick of your ubiquitous tentacles of selves!

SUN: (*laughing*) You and I are cut from the same cloth. (*Teasing a cloud, the sun swallows the sick man whole. Another man in his early forties drags himself and a wooden bench into the shadow.*)

SUN: No need to fret, my tinted friend. See, your food is served. (*Shade hesitates.*)

ACT II *Another man under a tree, reading. Something murky like Newtonian fluid has lodged in his chest, weighing him down, buoying him up. Distracted by the page, he locks his eyes on the gull on the chimney pot. The wind tastes of roses and manure.*

SUN: If you don't take him, I will.

SHADE: (*tongueless and murmuring*) He's reading Louise Glück.

SUN: So?

SHADE: Didn't you hear? She said the poem is a revenge on loss. And I'm nothing but loss. (*The sun too hesitates while spilling over the parking lot.*)

SHADE: (*twitching its fingers*) Shall we spare him then? (*The man looks up beyond the clouds for proof but the seagull has already taken off from the roof.*)

SUN: (*clearing its throat*) I am not afraid of *glück*. (*And opens its wide blue mouth.*)

ACT III *Outside the book. The man walks into the dark yew hedge waiting. And waiting.*

GERANIUMS IN MAY

While others sit on the windowsill
cloud-watching, I give birth
to geraniums in May in the chill

though I haven't a clue what it means
to be alive again – for what it's worth –
or to be blind to the multi-faced screens.

All my life I've wanted to be invisible,
not prized, yet my orange-scented babies
cry for recognition, for the indivisible

joy of singing *Fuck, I love this world.*
They love it too: tortoiseshells, goldfishes.
Love, like rhyme, is a big word.

There are bigger ones like geraniums
in May, not last or next but *this* May
as they explode everywhere, like uranium.

MANY JUNES

Something bad happened.
At the table still zingy with basil
you drew back and opened
your heart to the sour-milk storm
in our heads beyond counsel.
Nothing heavy, just plain facts
slid through the tongue
converting loss to some form
of chaos.
                    My eyes tasted salt and herbs.
Papery purple and sun-proud, it was the young
sage, not a Death's-head hawkmoth hovering
sheepishly above us, that broke me.
The many Junes we had, and might still have.
Our time-equation expanded as you
added this, added that, the could-haves
and couldn't-haves.
                                        I didn't know how
to subtract that from this, the colours from the frame,
our days so complete it seemed a shame
to be divided, not multiplied. The sun was strong.
Almost too strong. What was that thing bugging
us? This living once? I took the ink clouds
from your frazzled hair, and all I could think of
was rain.

ALL THESE LINES

All these straight lives
fall from the sky like lines
of unkinked ink crisscrossing
in a gorge famous for rain.
The pass is difficult still.
Even the deer wear bells
warding off acrophobia.
The torrents are looking at us
for revenge, while we try crossing
the bridge with nine other men
but…but the crow-black,
smoky, obsidian, Dantesque
atmosphere is too beautiful
not to admire in moments
of great danger. It's pain
I worry about for us in the dark
descent. We'll get wet
for sure, without straw hats
or raincoats, and you know
I hate getting wet. The willow
isn't bothered by bad luck.
Hiroshige neither. After this hillock
what's next? A rain-shelter?
All these lines on my palms
bend and swerve with their own
intentions, qualms.
I want to straighten them:
these loud raindrops, those nuclei
of dust hurtling helter-skelter
down the sky.

THE ART OF READING

after André Kertész

The last book I read before I died sits idle at my desk next to a clay dove by the window where the sun stops the wind entering but the sycamore walks through my chest and I can't return to the page

Once I stole a book from a library in Paris where the eyes of oak beams stared at me like bullet holes

And once in Esztergom barefoot I pretended to be reading while examining my friend's leather boots

In Washington Square on April 18th 1969 I leaned against another oak next to a black man I fell in love with as he was reading Balzac and I forgot the lines in my hands

And it was indeed an angel dressed as a girl sitting on a high wooden stool at the backstage touching Bach's crotchets and smiling

Sometimes after I lost someone I let the Seine read me

And sometimes in autumn when the dead are yellowing the soil I placed my jacket among the leaves and tasted the print of newspapers

Once in Luxembourg Gardens Proust ignored me

On a train to Kyoto I saw my mother reading my novel and a nun reading my poetry but I wasn't on a train to Kyoto and she wasn't my mother and there was no nun

Against the shelf of oversized artbooks he pressed his penis against my thigh while my index finger was stuck between the pages

The poster said Paper Is Needed Now so I sat on a rough pile by the shopfront with my choc ice reading my favourite comic strip as the world turned upside down

Outside Raven Books on Fourth Avenue in a pile of second-hand discounts I found my first Emily who insisted that *Of nearness to her sundered Things / The Soul has special times*

Once I dangled my feet from the balcony and one of my shirts blew off the washing line and I wanted to slip inside it and button it up as it fell and hit the ground

My family was poor but my mother said in a library I would be rich like a king

Did you see St Jerome extracting a thorn from my paw and teaching me Greek

You took off your shirt and propped Murakami against the sun as vertebra by vertebra I traced the story of your childhood back to where we could have met each other had I been born thirty years earlier

Even though we've lived together for nearly twenty years and are always reading sometimes I can't read you at all which I guess is a good thing

One day when I'm old and you're no longer around I shall read on my own on a bench by the sea where the iron railings cast strong slanted lines on the sand and a curlew appears out of the blue because it is you

One night I dreamed of a dung beetle crawling up a spine and trying to move a Voltaire as if he was Sisyphus

Last night I dreamed of my mother reading on her deathbed and I crawled into the bed with her only to find that she had left and I was reading her book in a language I had yet to learn and suddenly the bell rang and I jumped up like Lazarus and started telling you something about myself in English

A cow glances over my shoulder and shuns the news in the manger

The page I can't return to walks through my chest like the sycamore as the wind stops the sun entering the window and I turn to clay after reading the last book in which I sit idle at my desk with a dove

IN THE PHOTOCOPYING ROOM

Side 1

I broke spines. Prose that spoke to me I fingered tenderly.
The hyper-theorised I shoved them facedown scholarly

onto a plain of glass placider than the brain. The lid dipped
like a sky collapsing, and as I pressed *Enter*, the script

and I set foot into a three-second coffin. An intimate smell
like flesh exposed to a candid heat, each photoelectric cell

kissing the pages, holding hands with the jet-black alphabets
blinded by the flash: word after word reproduced in the original insets,

double-paged, always serif. Outside, the spectre-bark horse-chestnut
was stripping down into the first-person singular. I was shut

inside the tofu-sized room, alone with compound sentences
and literary criticism on gender politics, wars and parentheses,

postcolonial guilt, why we laugh, why we cry and why,
despite every fallen thing at my heels, I *was* I,

an asynchronous copy of intimacy and failure:
if Love appears the hermit crab won't change its behaviour.

Side 2

The door opened and a hat arrived, guarding my tanker desk
like the second-person plural, as you cut and pasted a boatload

of A4 passages like an orchestral conductor of texts. You were tense
and pushed for time. *Can I help?* I asked

as if a hand was all chaos needed. You might have nodded
with words (I have no recall); nonetheless I sat down

flooded by *The Rime of the Ancient Mariner*, my throat
parched for the life within and abroad, as I saw Coleridge float

between us. *A speck, a mist, a shape.* I recognised you.
The wind was fiddling with the clock on the wall coated in a hue

of sun-dust, while every part of speech slid off the narrative
severed by our scissors and clung onto our Pritt glue sticks

as if we were playing Scrabble, showing the poem's comparative
reincarnations beyond a thousand thousand slimy words in the river Styx

where in time we would unlearn our country and forgive our mother tongue.
The room was too small for a double bed, too drafty for our lungs.

I put our finished pages on the auto-feed and saw them multiply
into the waves drawing the sea-sand in and out, like a reply

like the enamoured sound of the aurum-arrow travelling through time
and ribcages, jamming the machine as our breath rhymed, unrhymed.

SELF-PORTRAIT WITH BANANAS

All day I expose myself to vulnerability
changing my shirt from chalk to indigo
looking for a clouded light that speaks
to the blank walls and my face
with the right kind of ambiguity,
not timid or cocky, just the presence
of someone who writes at his own tempo,
ill at ease with his own physique.
He knows the lens will change his soul
but lets it.
                    Oh, to be a *he*, a supernatural
salamander breathing through his yellow skin,
and live amphibiously with pleasure and discipline!
There he is, shying away from the camera,
zapping up the wall like a lightning bolt,
turning white, then off-white, into the light
on the wall, cloudy, statuesque, invisible
yet clear as day. What is he frightened of?
He stays where he's found love.
Suddenly he grows spots and darts into a bowl,
sleeps peacefully with a hand of bananas.

GREEN RAIN

We heard it falling
at the edge of the wood

though the wood
was blunt and nothing fell
quite like rain.

It didn't slip
through the clamshell
of parched hands.

It was a sound
I misunderstood.

We stood dead quiet
at the edge of a word
wondering.

Was it a hornbeam?
Persephone?
Barochory?

YEAR OF THE RAT

Not to return. Earth's the right place for love:

Except this year I abandon the birches
and flee to another middle-aged
galaxy – rocky, aqueous, Earth-sized
but not Earth-bound – where indigo flamingos
make alpine nests the shape of globe artichokes
and six-legged giraffes lay moon-coloured eggs
in saffron mangroves found only on Kepler-186f
'where the grass is always redder on the other side.'
Can I leave the land of absinthe and avocado
and adapt to a life of amaranth and cochineal
where clouds are not accounted for?
With no tilt on the axis would it even have seasons?
But not to return? Even Odysseus returns.
Persephone speedily returns to the Japanese knotweed
and sakura. The sun too returns to our morning
embraces when my left arm slips underneath
your head like a pillow and we travel the day
like two peas in a pod. But I'm weary of repetition
of these long nights of truncated dreams
and prohibitions when my eyes meet the traffic-free
ink-black ceiling, and I ask *What on Earth…?*
What on Earth? Then a bird (wren or great tit)
sings 'Fuck you, fuck you' on the cut branches.
For thirteen days the Queen birch has been weeping
out the rain she drank when the heavens opened
for weeks in the run-up to the Year of the Rat.
The birch sap falls. On a concrete step a patch of algae
is thickening into a moss-dominion of zinc, sugar,
calcium and manganese, before everything dries up.

The moss dies and leaves the stone,
an off-white imprint of eroded flesh and failure.

I don't know where it's likely to go better.

HONG KONG, CHINA

在這個城市裡，每天總有這些那些，和我們默然道別，漸漸隱去。

西西《我城》

In this city, everyday there is this and that. Things quietly depart, gradually disappear.

XiXi, *My City*

MOTHER'S INK

somewhere in the pre-history of ink is reproduction
– Caitríona O'Reilly

Born I was, and wasn't.
She drew breath from the breath she'd lost
to phantom explosions inside her.
Three days, three nights, all breaths
and no food or sleep.

What other mothers had done she did,
re-staging the contractions until my departure.
I saw what she saw:
a cloud of messy flesh waiting at the gate
redder than ink.

The hard plastic on the suction cap.
My misshapen head.
What she remembered I remembered.
A cloudless day at 3 p.m.
and no ink was spilled as she kept herself to herself.

Now and then words escaped from her
bleached hands.
She knew I wanted ink greedily.
She fed it to me, dark milk diluted with water
that, when it touched a page, spread.

She knew it came from the clouds
hiding the teargas and bullets.
She only wanted good ink for me but feared what it meant.
I wanted just ink for her.
I wanted ink more than her.

RAW MATERIALS

Day 1

a friend of a
friend is
shuffled out
of a radio
show.
Another
mouth shut.
Another
man's
whereabouts
unknown.
His dual-
nationality
scrapped.

Day 2

a bookseller's
accused of
crowdfunding
a protest.
Evidence of
systematic
failure
destroyed.
Burberry is
boycotted by
some stars.
Government
tells fourteen
countries to
deny the
legality of a
passport.

Day 3

a law firm is
ordered to
disband
because they
defend a case.
A university
axes a photo
exhibition.

Day 4

someone
suspends a
talk show,
someone
cancels a
documentary,
someone bans
the Oscars,
someone
restricts
someone's
access to
something
official.

Day 5

another man is
heard and
charged. A
law amended.
Police
empowered.
Election
candidates
screened.

2047: A HONG KONG SPACE ODYSSEY

for my sister

> *Bowman: Open the pod bay doors, HAL.*
> *HAL 9000: I'm sorry, Dave. I'm afraid I can't do that.*
> *– 2001: A Space Odyssey*

I too can't open that door, can't lend a hand, can't.
Two years from being a septuagenarian. Time never
elegises. We keep waiting, my sister and I, at the door.

It isn't a human error but something more systematic
like an army of red dots watching and listening.

'Let's talk to the leaves,' she says, 'they'll have answers.'

So I conjure up from Project Gutenberg *the sniff of green leaves*
and dry leaves, hopeful green, green intertinged, the dusky
green of the rye, pale-green eggs in the dented sand, dark
green lobsters... She full-stops my lips with a finger.

I fast-forward the rest of the 45 green occurrences
in that mighty book of Mr Whitman.
Other colours have no place in our Kingdom of Red.

'Don't hyper-process the past,' she says, 'they can detect
nostalgia, even the literary kind.' I shake my head
and throw a pen into space. It falls flat on the ground
opening up into a well that returns a sound like water.

'Don't waste your gravity quota, Kit. You'll regret it.'

INTERMISSION

Do you remember you stole Mum's lipstick?
Do you remember the red spread like a virus
on your three-year-old mouth? Do you remember
next to the lipstick a small thing sealed in paper?
Do you remember I asked you not to open it?
Do you remember those bright, shiny things
inside the wrapping paper and how I screamed?
Do you remember the blades? The blood
coating your mouth, slightly scented by the red
pigment only found in Chanel lipstick?
Do you remember I sat you by the window
to show you the clouds over Victoria Harbour
in the distance? Do you remember counting
those glass and steel monoliths across the water
from our own monolith? Do you remember
how long it took the blood to congeal?
Do you remember it was 1985, one year after
the Joint Declaration was signed by Deng
and Thatcher? Do you remember those tanks
on the television? Do you remember the two
indistinguishable eras of face masks? Do you
remember the writing on the Lennon Walls?
Do you remember being Blue or Yellow,
or both, or none? Do you remember what happened
afterwards? Do you remember those complex
variations of green, and how suddenly,
perhaps it was the wind, perhaps algorithms,
a wide gap opened up between two leaves of grass
and the sun stabbed straight into our eyes?
Do you remember how to remember
and disremember? Do you remember me?

STORIES FROM THE NORTH-WESTERN PROVINCE

Let's praise the eye
wired at the corner shop
selling lemons
and chickpeas to a spy

who likes chickpea salad
but locks up the boy
whose mother makes
the best chickpea salad

in Kashgar because a job is a job
like soldiers of army ants
from a penal colony
facing a mob

Let's praise the eye
hovering stealthily
over new concrete buildings
reporting from the sky

about a land of men
sitting on the ground
just sitting there interned
as in a pen

Let's praise the eye
and praise it to death
till there's nothing else
to praise but the eye

MNEMOSYNE

for Mimi

found her in Mong Kok
throwing herself into
the pepper smoke
lacrimae lacrimae

a million footsteps
shaped the water movement
as guns followed the eyes
of cameras

can't choose between
the goddess of memory
and forgetting which is
the alpha privative of thought

do you ever think of
me a blind spot a thorn
on your side a disremembered
joint declaration

not like flesh
and blood not like
immortalised slogans
on Lennon Walls

bound to be here
in the divided capital
of capital in the sticky
heat of chaos

they split
as the blue-dyed rain
stained the running
feet the kneeling feet

resist and keep
the city in the sovereign
present in the foreign
tongue

hunt him down find
him again on WhatsApp
hospital wards inside
tunnels over bridges

between flames and sirens
under shield and batons
which sheep from the flock
would you remove

dear friend why on earth
you jumped into the clouds
what worlds were there
to encode

THE SHAPE OF THE WIND

for Yoyo

You asked if I remembered my passport
my air ticket, the thirst
for elsewhere packed in my rucksack,
but we mustn't speak about the shape of the wind.

The wind is the shape of a rubber band
a root system tightly packed, a cloud
of tearful gas. The wind is travelling
though we mustn't speak about the shape of it.

Perhaps there is no answer as you search
everywhere for the different shapes,
the so-called mutability, the hug and the letting-go
of the wind that we mustn't speak of.

Perhaps there's a field of vision wider than memory,
perhaps it's the wind's shapeless thoughts
who blow you to a story of departures
though we mustn't speak about the shape of departures.

You asked if I remembered the missing
that had nameless shapes. And the gale-force wind
that carried diversions, divisions. But we mustn't speak
of the lawful intuitions that shaped the shape of the wind.

The shape of the wind is a passing rain
the eyes' salt crystals, a long-distance call
from where fear lodges. But we mustn't speak
of the wind or its shape, and everything in-between.

HOW TO BE A FERN

Blue-white then inky grey then hailstones
go pitter-patter on the glass.
The city I loved whose name I've erased returns
between me and the glass
as the thunder bends like saxophones
buried inside one of Keats's urns.
Give me a second chance, the city insinuates.
A legion of storm clouds evaluates
me. I was young, opened my heart
too soon and the wind tore it apart
just like that. Wind was never a city
except when it drained the blood,
stuffed silences like cotton wool
into my ears, eyes, nose, asshole,
mouth, and preserved what was left in me in mud
Silence is the city I still kiss, not reason
with. Many springs have swung by
and I keep kissing, unfurling my tongue
for the city in me I can't return
to isn't rain, wind, or glass. I'm no fern.
Tell me how to be and I'll learn
and unlearn.

HONG KONG AND THE ECHO

What do we know but that we face
One another in this place?
– W.B. Yeats, 'Man and the Echo'

HK. I loved my mountains, rivers and trees
long before towers and families, but if the only way
the sea can speak to the hills is through the moon
I will speak to you from the ink-dark
about the changing tides, the slow equivocal pain
of transition, how things are moving away
from the norm, the deceptive comfort
of a norm, the fading neon noises
on Mong Kok streets, the kind of blue and yellow
you'll only find in my heart, the Lion Rock spirit
and the endangered species named after me:
the grouper, cascade frog, incense tree.

Echo. *What do we know but that?*

HK. What's the meaning of life in numbers?
Although I count every second of mine
I remember nothing of those Crown-
appointed governors come and gone who said
nothing, did nothing, changed nothing.
What the promises lie in a red flag with five stars
shooting out from one bauhinia?
Twenty-six moon-calendars since I was re-unorphaned
I stray and obey like a tree, half-crown, half-root,
branching out and bedding in, each growth year

a scar tissue erased by the smudges
of shared stocks, fireworks, new railways and bridges.

Echo. *We face one another? We face one another?*

HK. What am I but the high-rise windows
reflecting the sun and the lives below?
Come, look into every single one
and find millions of homemade voices in an impasse,
in fissures, in boxlike existences
where one language is never enough.
High above I see black kites, sometimes white-bell
sea eagles gliding between glass and cliff,
drones and signals, eyeing the quick chance
while larks, thrushes and titmice are twittering
in bamboo cages, bird to bird, sharing
the captive sky with their distant counterparts
as one sun drops under the horizon
and a different one rises.

Echo. *In this place? In this place? In this place?*

JUNE

after Bei Dao

Wind is mouthing something in my mortised ear:
June

June stays blacklisted
while I hasten my disappearance

Please attend to the method of bidding
farewell

the audible respiration attached
to big words

Please attend to the interpretations of not-us:
plastic flowers blooming like umbrellas

on the open horizon or the left bank
of the dead

The great concrete square is extended
through writing

as in this moment
where my written characters take flight

where dawn is forged somewhere else
and a flag shrouds the sea

as ocean and her faithful bass speakers announce
June

PUI O

Lantau Island, Hong Kong, November 2019

After months of smoke and chase
after absorbing the errors and partitions
I want to see the sun setting
irresponsibly on Lantau Island
reddening the outgoing waves
too quick for the sand to grasp, as they swell
and retreat, regulating
the pulse like the peaks and troughs
of the mountainous backdrop
darkening against the duck-yolk yellow
that burns away my retinas
so I can see my home blind,
undivided, back in time
to the re-undiscovered fishing village
where the seafoam covers
my feet, withholding what can
and can't be changed
while I keep returning here to pick shells
and kick the ocean for
answers, and in these final moments
of the thin light dismantling
the day, nine water-buffalos, abandoned
paddy-field farmhands
stroll childishly along the edge to clean
their hoofs and replenish
lost salt, waiting for the heat to drop –
and suddenly I smell
the old ink brushing my neck,
thickening the sky into a void
and I shiver.

A LONG STORY OF MOON

○

Your killings emulsify in the brain.
First, make yourself a widow.
Second, leave your son in a pigsty.
Third, swim across Shenzhen Bay at night.
Fourth, find shelter in Lau Fau Shan (Mountain of Clouds and Currents).
Fifth, say *I'm a virgin and wasn't touched by the Japs.*

◗

Paperless, you were born again
as the maid of the tenth child in the Year of the Rat.
It was fear that produced the milk.
Strong milk it was
raising him to be a bodybuilder.

●

Your ivy-fingertips clung to the letters
steamed open and resealed, the missing
earrings, red pocket money.

A hive with two queens.

◖

The labyrinthine boxes in your room
opened to a skull or the skin
a snake had shed
(you were called a snake).

A tree-snake, herbivorous, leafy,
camouflaged against the past,
outliving the boy you breastfed
(my uncle who committed suicide).

○

Who would remember your name?
It had the word moon in it
like many lost women of your time.

◗

They tied you up in the nursing home
to stop you climbing out
the window.

The bruises flowered on your arms and hands.

●

I peeled red
grapes while Mother
stroked your hair

and temples
to calm your milky
brain.

◖

I didn't come back for your funeral.

○

Your grave is rarely visited
let alone swept
each year.

Cremated and enshrined far away
you bite my tongue and curse the wind
for speaking.

A STORY OF A LABYRINTH

Once – a spirit signalled – *there is more than one entrance*
to the skull – and walked in with a thread ——— as nimble
as water – surging into the grey grooves – and white
ridges of his mind devoted to steroids – *Wake your uncle* –
so I – climbed – up – to – his – dusky – attic – and found
naked muscles asleep – the reeds in his armpits – swaying
back and forth – as his breath touched – mine – Another
spirit entered – nudged my index finger – which started
drawing a doughnut – on his nipple – (I was six) – He
twitched – moaned – grabbed me – into – his arms –
tickling me – ears neck chest waist bum feet – his moves
unpredictable – like a boy discovering – an electric current
he had not yet learned – to touch ————————————
Over time – many spirits passed between us – suddenly
he was 39 and single – couldn't sleep – wouldn't sleep –
after fixing the wings of a 747 ———————— but was scared
of flying ———————————————————————— One day
———————a spirit ——————————————————
——————————————— contradicted ——————————
——————————————————————————— time ————
and rendered it inaudible – Everything – in the labyrinth
was wallpapered over – with images – of him duct-taping
the windows – drawing the curtains – super-gluing the door –
sealing the air off with a wet bath towel – throwing the key
in the bin ——————— What kind of a spirit – would summon
somebody – to tidy the house – turn off the electricity
phone water and gas – to lie in bed – to sleep – and let the charcoal
burn for four days – till his neighbours – picked up something
in their nostrils ——— A body – ballooned up – sunk – three
inches – into the mattress – was reported – in the news ——

——— Someone said – *the weight of the blood was the weight of water* – clouds rain rivers lakes estuaries the ocean – swept him away – but – I – knew – it – wasn't – water – or – spirit – It was him – looking in the mirror – taking the two lifelines in his hands – quashing them – and calling – *Minotaur* ——
————— *Minotaur* ——————————

THE ART OF DESCENT

I don't know why
  after years of separation
    her fear of descent

  into the world under
    still presses at my heels
      as if underness

    is a lake of vantablack
      ink everyone will plunge in
        get stained by

      and forget about living
        risks and defects
          like I'm doing now

        stealing the day from a climb
          up Easedale Tarn having dipped
            into the ice-water

          butt-naked as two buzzards
            patrolled the sun-clipped
              crags like cats

            bringing in a small creature
              at the edge of
                breath

              Mother
                unlike you who fell down
                  two flights of stairs

and lost your brain
to decades of migraine
I'm well and taking my time

held by my beloved
accompanied by friends on this steep
narrow path

where each step
grows firmer when my desire
to balance loses foothold

and time morphs
into muscles and waters
as we keep looking back

but fail to translate what
gravity and friction do
to the stream

making these stable
repeatable braids that knot
and unknot

on the surface
while I can't stop blinking and thinking
with Orpheus

BROKEN NOSED JIZŌ
the throat is also
an inkwell
Ocean Vuong

BROKEN NOSED JIZŌ

On Kumano Kodo where stones are eaten by clouds and moss
there stands
a pine

growing out of a rock circumventing another rock
whose face shelters
the lichen

The master carpenter was building a three-storied pagoda.

of lime, mint, sage, sea-foam and shamrock
indiscriminate as a clockwork
green

on which a Jizō whose head is part of the gone weather
was carved by a local
sculptor

Every day the apprentice prepared a lunch box for the master and took a small portion as an offering to the Jizō on the ridge.

who earned a good name but left the world unknown
like me and you and the many erased
in time.

I asked, 'God of the Earth Matrix, Earth Reserve, patron of hell-beings,
miscarriages and aborted
foetuses

The master assumed that the apprentice had been stealing from the lunch box.

if I gave you a new head, would your nose still be
broken for the good
deeds

I may or may not have done? With five births every
second are you sick
of us?'

His mouth cracked open, 'See – how you break your head
over ink, because someone you loved
died,

how you break your head for oil, naming a star, editing
a gene, over some land
or god,

see how you break it (*use a fist*) like this, and now
(*use a hammer*) like
this,

till your neurons spill through your poor bony skull,
running attit-longitudinally
wild

like an orchestra of frogs *qua-qua-qua-qua*-ing
from a spring waterhole, sperms head-
butting

through the slime-foam-cloud of eyelike eggs, impatient
to be born and unborn.
See –'

I aimed a stone at his nose and he stopped. I walked away
as ivy crept out of
my mouth.

One day he decided
to hide behind the
pine tree by the Jizō.

When he saw the
apprentice open the
lunch box, he rushed
out and struck him
in the face.

The apprentice fell
over, unharmed.

But the Jizō's nose
was broken, with
blood running down
the rock.

FROM THE YEMEN DATA PROJECT

1. September was the cruellest month, / with unguided cluster munitions / dispensing tennis-ball sized bombs / against soft-skinned / targets, but a shrapnel-spinning sky / is impartial as to the month.

2. Sirwah, a key stop on the incense route / where we found a plinth / from the Sanctuary of the Queen of Sheba / was the most bombarded / district, with 1101 airstrikes, and rising.

3. The pivot table shows 55 rows / beginning with the word 'civilian's': / farm, house, houses, truck, bus, boat, / gathering, vehicle carrying vegetables, / and Abdullah Al-Hassoni's house up in the hills / in Sihar levelled on 5th August 2015.

4. Other targets beginning with the letter C: / celebration stage, cement tanker, / cemetery, central jail, Central Organisation for Control / and Accounting, chicken farm, clinic, Cococola / factory, community college, cornfields (with sightings / of white drones), cotton processing factory, / court, crossing bridge, cultural hall, customs.

5. On the last Thursday of September 2015 / in a wedding ceremony in the port city / of Mocha on the Red Sea where the prized / olive-coloured coffee beans were shipped abroad, / 80 fatalities were triangulated, 32 women, 38 children, / but the time of day is unknown.

6. Most of the time the time of day is unknown / but if known it takes place at midday / when the sun bleaches away the fallen / concrete blocks, loose wires, burnt faces / or hands of those without faces.

7. 'When a report does not note whether / any fatalities occurred or not, or notes / that it is unknown whether fatalities / occurred at all, [it] defaults to coding 0 / as the fatality estimate.'

DEREK JARMAN'S GARDEN

You dwelt in impossibility.
First the waves spoke Shinglese but the shingle
didn't sing in a single tongue.
It clicked like dice rolling in cupped hands.
It hummed like the uranium in Dungeness.
Then, the moon fought for every speck,
every freckle, dimple, pimple, every facial expression
of the shingle lost to the sun's daily repossession.
But the moon was the most loved anthology
of repeatable failures. The simple equation
was not time times labour equals growth.
Take the troubled dog rose pressed against the flint,
betting its spiky luck
on a bank that catches a leeward damp.
Take the almond-white sloe flowers devoured
in a good year by browntail moths.
For some, home is less bothersome when they cease
to root in one place, say the dandelions
you were frightened of as a child, or the sea kale
with its psychedelic blue-violet-orange-green
red-indigo-yellow (it even has white flowers!)
spreading promiscuously. Delicious, though radioactive.
As to form, structure, and the instruments –
here the old handle of your rake and there the wires you sculpted –
they too are infectious like the music of rust;
that prompt metallic tick-tock ruling over us
busy old fools, as our bodies yellow slowly but surely
like mould lichen pollen
on this unlikely land where knowledge
is not concentrated in a single tree

but disseminated to every neighbourly shape and shade:
your blackwashed cladded fisherman's hut
of superior doors and numerous windows.
Your bright ochre window-frames filter
the heat of sunflowers, night-wind off the sea.

THE CHINESE IN SCHÖNBRUNN PALACE

Maria Teresa loved her tall white bluish urns
but was oblivious to bone exhumation

in which an aged corpse – skull, spine, ribcage,
pelvis and small toe's distal – is dug up,

washed with rice wine, painted with cinnabar
ink, so that oxygen can be breathed back

into the veins and muscles, only for the re-fleshed
to be reburied, like a stack of vintage nude

magazines treasured in tall white bluish urns
not dissimilar to those loved by Maria Teresa,

who couldn't have imagined seeing hundreds
of one-child-policy kids line up in bow-ties

and chiffon, crisp-white and cherry-pink, posing,
laughing, shrieking and tickling each other

like a colony of white flamingos drinking up
the yellow sun, standing on one leg, balanced

or slightly off-balance, as their parents
behold their future princes and princesses

on their screens, unaware that somewhere
a bell chimes ten times, pauses for three

seconds, then ten times again, as if time
    were stolen bones that could be exhumed

like these tired living bones (of man and wife) –
    drugged, not bothered about the formal

gardens, and now sitting on a bench –
    one puffing out cigarette smoke as the wolfish

Warfarin thins his blood, while the other
    busily licks her raspberry gelato spilling

over the wafer's edge onto her arm, breast,
    and abdomen, all steeped in Glimepiride:

this is the moment I enter and glime
    at them holding forth like partners in crime,

trespassing against their medical prohibitions
    under a stunted plain tree, oblivious to

their migratory son clicking a phantom shutter
    in quick succession, his Midas finger filtering

parenthood from warm to cool, original to silvertone,
    stealing the light from the sun, as if live colours

could be drained off from irises and everyone
    could take as much as they wanted for as long as it takes.

BUT WHO HAS WON?

after *Maggie Taylor*

In another version, Alice stays in her original form.
No scalability potion, just a girl holding an empty eggcup,
feet submerged in grey weedy waters, maybe an estuary,
maybe not. *It's a matter of time*, the dull foliage murmurs
in the background. She holds her lips after seven departed birds
have flown back from the blank and huddled around her.
The colours from *The Birds of America* scream out: *O it's scarlet!*
Or more like a dodo's! A flash of Xanadu on their breasts,
wings, irises: carefully preserved, songs downloadable.
Memory is a reproduction of loss, but who has won?
Her Prussian blue dress blends in with the lunisolar sky
though the blue looks all wrong. Too safe, too lifelike.
And the present tense? Who will dare speak the day?
The cumulus clouds think they have won. The pink knotted
fan coral branching out this season claims it has won.
What's in your other hand? A knife? The egg we've stolen?

OFFERINGS

The purple crocus dislikes sharing a shaded patch with the few snowdrops beheaded after a storm while a tree-fern harasses a silver birch swearing at the girl who stubs a cigarette butt on its trunk:

the Buddha watches and I watch what he sees, stuck between the Humanities Research Centre and Spring Lane Teaching Block, between a window-cascade and steel-panels of kindergarten-orange, wood and cement, ivy and a Coke Zero, knowledge and a hard place:

don't ask me what he looks like among hissing bamboo and lofty rhododendron, leaf-green and verdigris-green since 1984:

a gift from father to daughter donated to this sunless spot near a Fire Exit where depending on the season you can offer grief, a flower, clementine, penny, or bow:

a Primark pashmina wrapped over his shoulders, wish-letters asking for First Class Honours, and five cranes disguised as origami ripped apart by ten windy fingers:

March, the premature March, starts skinning the Year of the Pig

AFTER THE QUAKE

11th November 1855, 10 p.m.

The black-haired clouds that choked
the mouth of Arakawa River
weren't clouds. And the grey stubble

that grew on the morning snow
in the rice fields
wasn't only dead skin. The kids smothered

soot into their lampblack eyes
though footprints, a whole town of them,
had been eaten by the crows

that weren't crows. New names jostled
their way onto the crowded
noticeboard. And snow landed on the ink

dissolving. I didn't know what the bone-
coloured sky wanted but it kept begging me
to read it.

24th August 2016, 3:36 a.m.

It was your birthday. We kissed each other
good night. A dog barked and shook the lamp.
I turned off, left Aleppo behind with its limbs.
We slept with our heads elsewhere.

I woke and called the noise a ghost. You woke.
It threw us out of bed, naked. We crawled
under the IKEA table. Two wineglasses broke.
The ceiling fidgeted as the ground force mauled

the night for 30 seconds. We took our passports
to the open square. Sleepy kids in shorts
dozed like walnuts in their mothers' hands.
Men smoked busily by the newsstands.

After an hour we went back upstairs
and shut the door. It returned, but milder.
We lay in bed like stemless sunflowers.
A dog barked and we kissed each other.

WHAT YOU LOOK LIKE

Like courtroom sketches of the accused
devoid of all expression
your lipid membrane looks as lifeless
as the dark side of the moon
your spike glycoprotein red as roses
nimble as hands though electron-microscopically
speaking they aren't scarlet or vermilion
nothing to do with blood or lust
coronas or aggression but two interlocking
sub-units like a labyrinth of knitted wool
with endings and openings that give
your unmistakable binding grip
but also make you vulnerable
not unlike the flaws our maker forgot
when reproducing his own image
while in the background of the newsroom
sometimes you look like Yayoi Kusama's
infinite polka dots and sometimes like
Kandinsky's unfinished circles in boxes
or Seurat's pointillistic calm stolen from
the grey smoke and chimneys on the horizon
which still looks like our own horizon now
and although nothing any longer is impossible
with Athena's shield and spear
for months I've failed to commit your portrait
to memory as if what you look like is not
what you really look like when people
describe you generically as almond-eyed
with creaseless lids

bespectacled
black haired
funny nosed
masked
foreign

MOON SALUTATION

I sway
like Crusoe's palm trees
as the crescent-cut on my palm
hardens into manganese.
My mountain pose keeps the storm at bay
but fails to embalm
the daily risks. At home, on a soft mat
I move open-thighed,
inspecting the goddess inside
a man like me, phasing in and out,
bending my half-spent body
into a pyramid.
That day, Cairo tasted like wasabi
and I spotted her, white as a squid,
while the fireball
engulfed the crowds. She was cool,
invigilating.
Somewhere, another womb's ovulating
as I rotate and embody her display
and sway!

NOH MASK, YASEONNA

For nights on end I flirt with the moon, starving to earn
her thin gaze back
while the wind grows tall, sneering at my waistline.
It's my mother's face I want,
a desert face, squid-white.
The cancerous cells that kiss
her elongated back and finger her womb
with red bubbles I want.
It was my home. They stole it and I want it back.
Skin thin enough to see bone contours,
the collar a valley of wind, spine
ridges of the Great Wall
seen from space.
Hairs on blue veiny arms turn into feathers,
a girl Icarus whose mother was unknown.
She was beautiful – that I know.
Why eat when I can just breathe?
Time is minus-me on a mirror with Venus
razors. Trees, thickly September,
mock me
with leaves and nuts.
The only bearable thing is lightness.

EPIDAURUS

for Emily

Some nights, separated from the sea, my eyes open like a gate
without my brain in it

and the ink floods in through the sockets, dilating the pupils
while I wait

for Asclepius or someone like him with well-oiled ears licked
by a snake

to touch my dream in which I play all the Odysseuses yet to be translated
arguing with himselves

failing to hear his mother's cry from the dark field littered
with asphodels

and therefore the lines are abducted; so no reunion, no embrace,
nothing left but white bones

as in foreign catastrophes reported by the World Service
that trouble and soothe

us, adding weight to my eyelids as a storm gathers in Sole,
Lundy and Fastnet,

as if the sun, the sight of sea squills, the scent of pine, wild sage and oregano
alone could heal

our first and last loves, the shattered ice, burning hills, lost people of
Yemen and Rakhine –

but I'm wading in, catching the spring water with my mouth,
and taking my share of every single moment.

HOKKAIDO

It was summer in Hokkaido.
    The forest stole the wind
    and I swallowed my footsteps.
    Nobody came to the springs.
    Butt-naked I sat halfway
    through my life measuring
    this, that.
In Hokkaido it was summer.
    Everything was halved or merged.
    Half-cut fingers, half-foxgloves,
    a marrowbone-cum-cabbage white.
    The cloud-light moon, split.
    I talked to nobody about
    this, that.
Hokkaido in summer it was.
    Ants were carrying a caterpillar
    home. No bird arguing.
    Nobody said missiles crossing
    so I stayed. The night trees
    stole the seas, cancelling
    this, that.

ACKNOWLEDGEMENTS

I thank my early readers David Harsent, Sarah Howe, Caitríona O'Reilly, Alice Oswald and Adam Phillips for their close reading and encouragement. I thank Rachael Allen and Colette Bryce for time and support.

I thank Derek Mahon, XiXi, Ocean Vuong, Bei Dao, W.B. Yeats for their words, and Shakespeare for the dragon-cloud, Marianne Moore for her supernatural salamander. I thank Hokusai and Hiroshige, the ink-masters, and André Kertész for teaching me how to read. I thank Yoyo Sham for her voice behind 'The Shape of the Wind'. I thank Yemen Data Project for their invaluable work and the Armed Conflict Location & Event Data Project (ACLED) for the quote about fatality methodology.

The images in the book are the sheets of marble from Santa Maria dei Miracoli in Venice. I photographed them in April 2022, after two years of suspended animation during the pandemic.

I thank the editors of the following publications where earlier versions of these poems were printed: *Cha: An Asian Literary Journal*, *fourteen poems*, *Granta*, *Modern Poetry in Translation*, *Oxford Poetry*, *POETRY*, *Poetry Ireland Review*, *Poetry London*, *PN Review*, *The Guardian*, *The Moth*, *The Poetry Review*, *The Stinging Fly*, *Salmagundi*, 聲韻詩刊 *Voice and Verse Poetry Magazine*, and *World Literature Today*.

I thank the judges and Forward Ars Foundation for including 'Suddenly' in *The Forward Book of Poetry 2022* (Faber, 2021)

I thank Mary Jean Chan and Andrew McMillan for including 'Hokkaido' in *100 Queer Poems* (Vintage, 2022).

I thank Eddie Tay and Joshua Ip for including 'Pui O' as part of 'Hong Kong – Singapore Digital Travel Bubble' project during the 2021 lockdown, published online by *poetry.sg*. I thank Yeow Kai Chai for a memorable exchange.

I thank Ian Duhig for inviting me and including 'What You Look Like' as part of the project 'From Irish Fever to Chinese Flu: The Racialisation of Epidemics'. I also thank Anna Chen, Don MacRaild and the team at London Metropolitan University.

I thank Spencer Reece for including 'Epidaurus' in *Unamuno Festival Anthology* (Desperate Literature, 2019) and everyone at Desperate Literature in Madrid for their hospitality.

I thank Matt Bevis for being the warmest host at Keble College.

I thank the health professionals at Magnolia Centre of York Hospital and Malton Community Hospital for care.

I thank Helen Mort for selecting some of the poems in this book for Northern Writers' Award for Poetry 2022 and for New Writing North for their support, especially Will Mackie.

I thank John McAuliffe for expert editing, for time spent on pondering the ink, music, and comma together. I thank Michael Schmidt for believing in my poems, and everyone at Carcanet for bringing the book to light.

I thank Matt Turner, my indispensable agent for supporting me through thick and thin.

I thank my friends for being there: Adam Phillips, Amanda Lillie, Anna Armstrong, Brian Cummings, Caitríona O'Reilly, Emily Berry, Freya Sierhuis, Geoffrey Weaver, Hélène Lecossois, Hermione Lee, Jessica Murry, John Barnard, Judith Clark, Kabbie Ngo, Kate Weaver, Lionel Pilkington, Lorraine Ng, Michael Fend, Michelle Kelly, Mimi Ching, Nicoletta Asciuto, Polly Yuen, Spencer Reece, Teresa Kittler, Ziad Elmarsafy…

I thank Hugh, the closest reader I write to. Thank you for reading and responding, for our hugs and togetherness.